# Prayers before Confession

- **To the Holy Spirit**

  Holy Spirit of God,
  give light to my mind
  so that I can remember
  all my sins.

  Let me be sorry
  for them and tell them
  to the priest
  who takes the place of Jesus.

- **To Mary Our Mother**

  Holy Mary, Mother of God,
  make my heart
  ready for Confession.

  Help me to be
  a true child of God
  and keep me close to Jesus.

# This book belongs to

Sarah Hanson

---

Date 9-23-00

## Presented by

Laurene & Grandma

# Going to
# Confession

## HOW TO MAKE A GOOD CONFESSION

By
### Rev. Lawrence G. Lovasik, S.V.D.

*Divine Word Missionary*

NIHIL OBSTAT: Daniel V. Flynn, J.C.D., *Censor Librorum*
IMPRIMATUR: Joseph T. O'Keefe, *Vicar General, Archdiocese of New York*

# THE SACRAMENT OF PENANCE

IN the Sacrament of Penance
Jesus comes to forgive your sins
and brings peace with God
and with the Church,
which is hurt by your sins.

Jesus loves children.
He makes them happy
by keeping them close to Himself
through the Sacrament of Penance.

# TO RECEIVE THE SACRAMENT OF PENANCE

To receive the Sacrament of Penance you must:

1. Find out your sins.
2. Be sorry for your sins.
3. Make up your mind not to sin again.
4. Tell your sins to the priest.
5. Do the penance the priest gives you.

# 1. EXAMINATION OF CONSCIENCE

Before going to confession,
quietly examine your conscience
so that you can find out
the sins you may have committed
since your last good confession.

Your conscience will remind you
if you have offended God
by committing any sins.

Ask the Holy Spirit to help you.

"Come Holy Spirit
and help me
to find out my sins
and to be really sorry for them."

# Finding Out Your Sins

You find out your sins
by remembering the Commandments of God,
and asking yourself
how you have disobeyed God.

By going to confession often
children learn to know how they offend God by
    sin,
and find peace and joy by seeking God's forgive-
    ness.

# Questions You Ask Yourself
## *About God*

### THE TEN COMMANDMENTS

**GOD SPEAKS:**

1. "I, the Lord, am your God, you shall not have other gods besides Me."

- Did I miss saying my morning or night prayers?

- Did I miss saying a prayer during other times of the day?

You honor and worship God by being faithful in saying your daily prayers.

## *About the Holy Name of God*

G

GOD SPEAKS:

2. "You shall not take the name of the Lord, your God, in vain."

● Did I use holy names, like "Jesus," and "God" when I should not have used them?

When children get angry and fight they may easily use the name of God and Jesus. This is sinful.

# About Sunday

3. "Remember to keep holy the sabbath day."

- Did I miss Mass through my own fault on Sunday or a Holy Day?

- Did I misbehave during Mass?

You keep Sunday holy by going to Holy Mass. It is a serious sin to miss Mass through your own fault.

## *About parents*

## 4. "Honor your father and your mother."

- Did I disobey my parents or teachers?
- Was I mean to them?
- Did I answer back?
- Did I make fun of my parents or old people?

You honor your father and mother by obeying them.

9

## *About being kind*

## 5. "You shall not kill."

- Did I hate anyone?
- Did I do anything mean to anyone?
- Did I let myself get angry?
- Did I quarrel and fight?
- Did I wish anything bad to anyone?
- Did I make anyone sin?

Jesus said that if we forgive others, God will forgive us. Confession helps us to forgive others.

# *About being pure*

GOD SPEAKS:

6. "You shall not commit adultery."
9. "You shall not covet your neighbor's wife."

- Did I do anything that was really impure?
- Was it alone or with others?
- Did I willingly keep impure thoughts in my mind?
- Did I sin by using impure words?
- Did I sin by looking at or reading anything impure?
- Did I sin by talking about or listening to anything impure?

Jesus said,
''Blessed are the pure of heart,
for they shall see God.''

To be pure means to be without sin.
The Sacrament of Penance takes away your sins
and helps you to avoid evil.
If you are in God's grace—free from sin—
you will be truly happy.

# *About being honest*

7. "You shall not steal."
10. "You shall not covet anything that belongs to your neighbor."

- Did I steal anything?
- Did I keep anything that did not belong to me?
- Did I damage what belongs to someone else?

Bobby stole some of Susie's lunch and made her very unhappy. He offended God by being selfish.

## *About being truthful*

**GOD SPEAKS:**

8. **"You shall not bear false witness against your neighbor."**

- Did I tell any lies?
- Did I tell mean things about anyone?
- Did I like to listen to unkind talk about others?

When you study your Catholic religion you will learn to tell the truth and to love all people in your words.

14

# 2. BEING SORRY FOR SIN

Before your sins can be forgiven,
you must be sorry for them,
because by your sins
you have offended God, your
  Father,
and because Jesus suffered on
  the cross for your sins.

In confession you thank Jesus for having
died on the cross so that your sins may be
forgiven.

# 3. DESIRE NOT TO SIN AGAIN
## An Act of Contrition

MY God,
   I am sorry for my sins
   with all my heart.

In choosing to do wrong
   and failing to do good,
I have sinned against You
   whom I should love above all things

I firmly intend, with your help,
   to do penance,
   to sin no more,
   and to avoid whatever leads me
   to sin.

Our Savior Jesus Christ
   suffered and died for us.
   In His name, my God, have mercy.
   Amen.

O my God,
 I am heartily sorry
for having offended You,
and I detest all my sins,
because of Your just punishments,
but most of all,
because they offend You, my God,
who are all-good
and deserving of all my love.

I firmly resolve,
 with the help of Your grace
 to sin no more
 and to avoid the near occasions
 of sin. Amen.

# Father, Forgive Me

OUR Father in heaven:
please forgive me
for the things
I have done wrong;

for being greedy
and wanting the best for myself;

for angry words and bad temper;

for making other people unhappy.

MY loving Father, I love You
because You are so good.
I am sorry for all my sins
and all I have done to hurt You.

With the help of Your grace,
I will try to do better
that I may please You
and show You my love.

Make me one with You always,
so that my joy may be holy.

Let me honor You by helping others
for the love of You.

Give me the peace and joy
that lasts forever.

The priest is sent to give you God's love
and forgiveness, but it is Jesus who forgives
your sins and sends His Holy Spirit once more
to your soul with new grace to lead a holy life.

# 4. TELLING YOUR SINS TO THE PRIEST

THE Catholic Church teaches,
   that the Sacrament of Penance
brings you God's forgiveness
for the sins you committed
after Baptism.

You receive God's forgiveness
through the priest
who has the power
to take away your sins.

He has that power
because Jesus gave that power
to His Apostles
and to His Church
in the Holy Priesthood.

# How To Make Your Confession

1. Make the sign of the cross.
2. Tell the priest when you made your last confession.
3. Confess your sins.
4. Listen to what the priest tells you.
5. Say the Act of Contrition.
6. Thank the priest.

Jesus said that the angels in heaven are happy when a sinner repents of his sins.

In confession Jesus comes to forgive
your sins and sends his Spirit to your
soul with grace and strength.

# 5. WHAT TO DO AFTER CONFESSION

After confession:

1. Say the penance the priest has given you.
2. Thank God for forgiving your sins.
3. Ask God for the help you need to keep from offending God.

Thank God for the graces of His Sacrament and ask for His help to lead a good life.

# Father, Thank You for Peace

HEAVENLY Father,
   by dying on the Cross for love of us
Your dear Son Jesus
brought peace to the world
by taking away our sins
and giving us your forgiveness.

As a Catholic child I receive
   this peace and forgiveness
   in the Sacrament of Penance.

I thank You for your mercy to me
   and to all who are truly sorry
   for having offended You.

Help me to use this sacrament often.

May the power of Your love
   given to me in this sacrament
   guide me in all I do
   to please You in all things.

Father, thank You for Your peace.

# WHAT JESUS DOES FOR YOU IN THE SACRAMENT OF PENANCE

When you go to confession you receive a sacrament which Jesus Himself gave us the evening of His resurrection on Easter.

1. Jesus gives you more sanctifying grace, which makes your soul more holy and beautiful. It is God's own life and presence in your soul.

2. Jesus gives you more sacramental graces—actual graces—which give you the light to see and the strength to do what is good and to avoid evil.

3. Jesus helps you to love God, and people for the love of God, because this is His Great Commandment.

4. Jesus helps you to make up for your sins in this life that you may die in His grace and be united with Him in heaven forever.

Through frequent confession Jesus gives
you His own peace and joy.

IN the Sacrament of Penance
Jesus helps you to be holy
because He sends His Holy Spirit
to your soul
with grace and strength
to live a better Christian life
and to keep away from sin.

True sorrow for sin
brings back the grace of God
if you have lost it by a serious
or mortal sin.

If you have committed a serious sin
you must receive the Sacrament of
    Penance
before receiving Holy Communion.

Through frequent confession Jesus unites you with Himself and also with the Father and the Holy Spirit, and helps you to be holy.

# THANK YOU, MOTHER MARY

MARY, Virgin Mother of Jesus,
you are my dear Mother, too.

I thank you for leading me to Jesus
that He might take away my sins
in the Sacrament of Penance.

Keep me from all sin
that I may love Jesus with a pure heart
as you always did.

I give myself to you
that you may protect me
and lead me to Jesus, your Son,
in Holy Communion.

May I always enjoy
the help of your prayers,
for you bring us life and salvation
through Jesus Christ your Son.